HOW TO HR

Essentials for
Managing a Solid Team

SHAYNA ROBINSON

HOW TO HR
Essentials for Managing a Solid Team

ISBN 978-1506-911-97-7 PBK
ISBN 978-1506-911-98-4 EBK

April 2024

Published and Distributed by
First Edition Design Publishing, Inc.
P.O. Box 17646, Sarasota, FL 34276-3217
www.firsteditiondesignpublishing.com

ShaynaRobinson@HowToHR.Org

Cover designed by Shayna Robinson Edited by Shayna Robinson

To my son. I love you.

To my HR tribe, small business owners, and new managers; I made this book with you in mind!

Contents

What's The Point

What's the Point?

As Simon Sineck would say, find your "why". Leading with "why" helps guide business decisions. As a HR professional, manager or business owner; think about your why when it comes to people management. You want your team to enjoy where they work. Why? Because it makes collaboration on projects easier, communication flows smoother and the business is in a better position to retain A players. Having a solid team means people enjoy the work they do, with the people they work with, at the place the work at. Outside of family; as a manager you directly impact work dynamics, pay, and livelihood. That I why it is important to provide people the opportunity to use their skills and creativity while they add to company profits, productivity, and competitiveness.

Empowering people to do their best work means providing people with the tools, technology, and leadership to excel. This book will be your guiding force for enhancing the employee experience while leading with confidence and clarity.

3 Pillars

Every business has three pillars that serves as the foundation. To understand the essentials of managing a solid team you must first understand the three foundational pillars in every business.

- Talent management
- Risk and workplace safety
- Compensation and benefits

People need compensation and benefits that allow them to care for themselves, a workplace that is safe and a team of collaborative people they can work with. After all, without people there is no business or team. Hiring quality talent is not just about creating a good work environment. Hiring the right talent can also improve your company culture. When you have a solid team who believe in your company's mission and values, they are more likely to work well together and create a positive work environment.

People also have the power to impact the company's bottom line. A competitive compensation and benefits package can help retain talent and keep companies financially solvent.

According to a report from Hiscox Insurance,1 in 5 small businesses will face employment related administrative charges. To mitigate these risk, employers must be proactive with upskilling and reskilling talent, understanding external factors, and consistently analyzing data.

The Dream Team

Dreams Turned Reality

Your dream team doesn't have to be a dream. Be creative and intentional in where you find talent and how you build your team. It can be overwhelming, so let's clarify the chaos. Here are a few key areas to consider for your recruiting and hiring needs.

- What job boards do you use? Are they attracting diverse talent?

- Are you networking at schools, community events, and with local organizations to find a mix of talent?

- Are recruiters, hiring managers, and HR in constant communication?

- Is onboarding informative, welcoming, and fun?

- Is our application process chaotic or conducive?

- Are we asking the right interview questions?

- How do we provide workers with the tools, resources, and insight they need to do their best work?

- Is our recruiting technology working for us or against us?

Small Action, Big Reward

It is the little things that makes a candidate stand out; whether it's sending a follow-up thank you note or sharing a fun fact about themselves to highlight personality. Well it's also important for employers to stand out to applicants. Be tedious and detailed from the very beginning of your recruiting process. Where you recruit is just as important as how you recruit. Aside from qualifications, work schedule, and experience; think about additional standards to attract solid talent.

- In 2- 3 sentences how would you decide your company culture? What perks do you offer employees?

- What opportunities do you provide for advancement and career growth? Why would people get excited about this role?

- Is your interview process virtual or in person?

- Is this a temporary remote position that will transition on site eventually?

These details matter...a lot.

The First Date

A job interview is like a first date. Let me explain this carefully so there is no confusion (or lawsuits). Remember the first time you went on a date? You made sure you had good conversation topics and made a lasting impression. As an interviewer, you want to make the company shine and intrigue the person to come back. Remember, you are looking for someone that can be a great add to your company. Avoid hiring someone that is exactly like you. Instead, find out what type of person would be best in that position and for the company. Questions to consider:

- Would this person work well under pressure?

- Does this person value autonomy, teamwork, or both?

- Can this person work well independently in a remote environment?

- Does this person have the ability to do the job exceptionally well based on the job specifications?

- Why are you hiring? Is this a new position, are you expanding or backfilling a role?

- Do you have the capacity to manage a new team member well? If not, what priorities do you need to arrange or delegate for this to happen?

Unicorns Aren't Real

Stop looking for unicorns, unicorns aren't real. The perfect candidate does not exist. You may be saying "but Shayna, why does the perfect candidate not exist?" Because people are people and we all have strengths and weakness. The person could be great in their role but chews with their mouth open during lunch (yikersss!).

Instead, hire people that are unique, creative and passionate. This means you have to do your part in interviewing exceptionally well.

Questions that may seem innocent can be discriminatory in reality. Asking if someone has kids, has ever used illegal drugs and salary history can all be discriminatory. Asking discriminatory questions can lead to costly lawsuits and bad press. We want to avoid that!

Interview notes are important but be careful what you put in writing. Notating physical characteristics such as race, hair color or appearance can be discriminatory, even if you are trying to paint a visual picture for memory.

- Review candidates based on skills and qualifications needed to successfully complete job duties. Remember, there is more than one way to perform a task. As a people manager, it is your responsibility to work together with potential team members who may need reasonable accommodations.

- Prepare a list of interview questions in advance. Ask candidates applying for similar roles, similar questions. This creates consistency and structure in your interviewing process. This also allows you to accurately compare candidates.

- Avoid assumptions or any personal opinions. Stick to facts, not opinions.

Best Practice

Interview Best Practices

- Be creative. Ditch the typical boring interview questions and think outside the box. Think about the ways people get work done, the team dynamic technology used, career paths and company culture.

- Present a fun challenge so candidates are in situations to show their true selves. In interviewing for a HR consultant role, part of the interview process involved a roleplay scenario where I presented a workplace technology feature to a small business owner.

- It's the unwritten workplace rules that make the difference. Ask the candidate what type of work environment they thrive in.

- Document reasons why a candidate was selected over others. If compliance ever comes into question, you have documented credible reasons why candidates were not selected compared to others.

Variety is Best

A variety of sources for quality candidates is a must. If you have a new opening within your team, wouldn't it be great if your current team members bragged about it. Word of mouth is one of the best recruiting sources. Applicants are applying with a positive mindset because of the great things they learned from internal team members. When you go above and beyond for your team, they go above and beyond for you.

In addition, you can spread the word about job openings through your LinkedIn or connecting with local human service organizations. Job boards can be beneficial but those one-on-one personal connections make a big impact on trust and relationship building from the beginning. Building a talent pool is one of the most proactive tactics in finding the right people. Instead of waiting until you have an open position, you can recruit in advance.

Leverage a variety of resources to create a broad talent pool. Internships are a great way to find talented employees who appreciate the college credits and experience they gain. At a previous company, we hired a law student who provided some entry-level legal assistance. It was a win for the student who gained experience and for the company who was able to find someone to do administrative legal work for a reasonable price. In addition, when employers connect with interns, they gain a trial period for finding brilliant minds who can join the team upon graduation.

Times Ticking

The average attention span is 8.25 seconds. Capture candidates' attention in your job ads. Rather than simply highlighting your company culture, create job postings that speak to the open position.

Consider Soba Noodle Shop in Japan, which struggled to find new employees. They didn't change the position but reworded the job ad which attracted qualified candidates that ultimately led to a new hire!

The first job ad read;

"Work at a beloved, long-standing 120- year-old restaurant".

After rewording the job posting they came up with this winner;

"Work at a place where you don't have to speak to anyone all day"

That's definitely going to catch applicants' interest. Use creativity to help attract quality talent.

Highlight your company and culture in a few sentences, explain the details of the position, and definitely keep it fun! The hiring process for the employee and employer can be a lot so keep it light and fun when you can.

Trust

*Because being a decent human is the real **flex**.*

Trust is an important message to convey in job postings. Employees want reliable honest communication and the ability to trust the company's processes. Make the application process as smooth as possible. This means easy to use technology and communication.

When interviewing, be real when talking to candidates in context of work-life harmony, management style, and external factors that impact employees. If there is a major external event that impacts the company, discuss how it is being handled internally. Think about the safety concerns candidates had during COVID-19.

Easing those concerns during the interview process builds trust and safety which is a key pillar for any business. Even if you do not have all the answers; be transparent about your efforts.

Trusting Your Team

Establishing trust is just one part, trust must also be maintained. According to a study by the Bureau of Labor and Statistics (BLS), employees who feel their organization supports work-life balance also have similar outlooks on trust.

Here are some ways you can start create and maintain a culture of trust.

- **Connect**. Connect with employees consistently for one-on-one meetings so you have a solid understanding of projects, stressors, barriers and more.

- **Support**. Having self-guidance is great, but some employees like and need the extra support. Before giving autonomy, ensure you give it to someone who will succeed- not someone who will feel abandoned. Before hiring, determine if the role is more collaborative, independent or a mix and ask interview questions to determine if that person would succeed in the role.

- **Communication**. Set clear expectations and make sure they are understood. Talk about mistakes. If you mess up, own up to it. Saying sorry is not a sign of weakness but true leadership. Now employees can easily communicate their mistakes because of the level of trust.

Rise of the Gig Economy

What's in a Name?

Gig Workers VS Employees

Despite this famous line used by William Shakespeare to convey that the naming of things is irrelevant; naming is quite relevant with worker classification.

Contractors (also referred to as gig workers) and employees are both workers, but their classifications are very different. Contractors have more independence but employees have more protections.

Gig workers can definitely be part of your dream team. However, there are some major differences when employing gig workers versus employees. Let's discuss this more in the next section.

New Rules

The modern career path has changed and will continue to evolve. It is crucial for businesses to know how they can benefit from the entrepreneurial workspace. The gig economy isn't new, but the pandemic forced people to find a way to make means. During the COVID-19 pandemic, the gig economy skyrocketed at full speed. With good partnerships, employers can collaborate with niche experts to help exceed business goals and add competitive value.

Gig workers are not a replacement for talented in-house employees. Instead, gig workers are freelancers and contractors that can provide expertise to specialized projects. In return this is freeing up your employee's time to work on projects aligned with their job duties and skills.

Gig workers also help businesses remain competitive and agile during times of less stable growth. Small businesses can meet demands without hiring employees and taking on the risk of having full time employees before cash flow is consistent.

Good Gigs

The gig economy is and will continue to be part of the workforce. This means employers have the opportunity to be creative in preparing how to partner with gig workers.

How will your organization create an environment that provides gig workers autonomy while feeling included?

Opportunities.
Think about potential opportunities your company may find with gig workers. What projects would be best to outsource, require specialized skills or would save time/money if completed by another worker?

Support career development.
Just because gig workers may not be direct employees, career growth and development are still important. Provide opportunities for projects that allow gig workers to use their current skills while establishing new areas of knowledge.

Tech, tech, tech!
Prepare for the future. COVID-19 has proved that employees can work well almost anywhere. Teams are connecting using tools like webcams, zoom, and basecamp. Use technology to host virtual meeting and connect with a array of talent. Technology has empowered a world where we can work anywhere by removing geographical borders and communication barriers disperse teams.

Set Clear Expectations
Create an organized list of all project details from start to success and what resources are needed to achieve goals.

Detailed Insight
Provide workers with detailed insight and information to successfully complete projects. Gig workers do not need the

same type of onboarding and new hire training as employees, but details and timelines are still important.

Get to Know Your Workers
You will know less about gig workers since they are not permanent employees. Take the time to get to know your workers and their interest in certain jobs so you can gauge interest for future projects.

Stay Connected
In today's blended workforce you may have a gig worker that is virtual or working with your virtual team. Make sure gig workers have temporary access to necessary technology. Whether it's tools like basecamp for managing projects or visibility to certain documents.

Don't Micromanage
Micromanaging is rarely good, especially for contractors. Gig workers appreciate their autonomy. Good gig workers know how to manage themselves; just make sure clear project instructions are provided. Partnering with gig workers is also a way to free up time. If you need to micromanage you should reconsider partnering with that gig worker.

Pay
Money is the motive. Make sure you have a simple way to pay gig workers. Ensuring workers have a clear understanding on payment dates, measurables/milestones for payment and what happens if work isn't acceptable or correct. Payment terms are just as important as payment amount and should be decided before a project begins

> *DID YOU KNOW: Statista estimates that by 2027, about half of the U.S. population will have engaged in gig work. Today, 35% of U.S. workers are involved in the on-demand gig economy.*

Part of the team
Gig workers should feel like they are part of the team with the projects they are doing. Yes, there are fine lines you have to

stay within to maintain compliance in a contractor/employer work relationship.

Still, gig workers should be involved by giving their opinion, insight, and expertise.

Offering gig workers company swag and optional invitations to team meetings can help you stand out as an employer and build long lasting relationships with gig workers.

Inclusive Gig Economy

When managed correctly, gig work, like self- employment, generally enables people with disabilities to gain experience, training, and ability to live an everyday life. The Equal Employment Opportunity Commission (EEOC) jurisdiction does not extend to independent contractors, but section 504 of the rehabilitation states best practices for employers.

- Help gig participants keep track of expenses for their gig taxes. Apps like shoeboxed can be used to scan receipts and create expense reports.

- Help gig workers have insight on criteria that would exceed income levels that invalidate state, federal, and health support.

- Having all training, documentation, support, websites, and apps comply with WCAG 2.1 Level AA to make sure no one is excluded because they use assistive technology.

Blurred Lines

According to the IRS, the following three common law rules help determine whether a worker is truly a independent contractor. Answering "yes" to any of these questions can mean the worker is an employee and not a contractor. Employers must consider all these factors when determining worker classification. Sometimes (actually a lot of the time) the lines get blurred. There is no "magic" or set number of factors that 100% determine if a worker is a contractor or an employee. The key is to review the entire relationship and consider the extent that best determines worker status. Remember to document those factors just in case you need to present them in the future.

1. **Behavioral**: Does the company control or have the right to control what the worker does and how the worker does his or her job?

2. **Financial**: Are the business aspects of the worker's job controlled by the payer? (these include things like how worker is paid, whether expenses are reimbursed, who provides tools/supplies, etc.)

3. **Type of Relationship**: Are there written contracts or employee type benefits (i.e. pension plan, insurance, vacation pay, etc.)? Will the relationship continue and is the work performed a key aspect of the business?

Employee		Contractor
Working for someone. Has a manager/boss.	**BOSS**	Complete autonomy. Own boss.
Paid hourly, salary, or piece rate.	**MONEY**	Typically paid in installments or when project ends.
Uses employers' tools and resources. Must attend mandatory training and meetings.	**RESOURCES**	Provides own tools and resources. Contractors typically have advanced knowledge; Training is not required.
Employer decides how and when work will be performed.	**DECISIONS**	Works on own terms and decides how they will perform work.
Employer assigns task to individual.	**SCHEDULE**	Contractor decides what work they will do as long as they complete the project.
Work is essential to the business. (A restaurant hiring a chef is different from a retailer contracting with a chef).	**ESSENTIAL**	Work is not essential for the business. Not a typical job role or duties.
Ongoing relationship.	**RELATIONSHIP**	Work ends after project is complete.

There are pros and cons when it comes to hiring employees or contractors. While hiring contractors can have less employer responsibility do not try to take a shortcut by hiring contractors for financial savings. This can cost you big in the long run.

Misclassifying employees can impose cost up to $25,000 per misclassification!

The gig economy is here to stay, but it will not be fully available to people with disabilities until solid steps for inclusion are paved.

Employment Laws & Regulations

Age is Just a Number

The **Age Discrimination in Employment Act (ADEA)** was passed to prevent discrimination in the workplace on the basis of age. The Age Discrimination in Employment Act (ADEA) prohibits age discrimination against people who are age 40 or older. It does not protect workers under the age of 40, however some states have laws that protect younger workers from age discrimination. It is not illegal to favor an older worker over a younger one, even if both workers are age 40 or older.

Discrimi HATE

Protected class refers to certain groups of people protected by anti-discrimination laws. This includes women, older workers, minorities, and people with disabilities. It is important to avoid disparate treatment which happens when people of a protected class are discriminated against. **Discriminate** is **discrimi-hate**.

Do The Right Thing

The **Americans with Disabilities Act (ADA)** prohibits discrimination against a qualified individual with a disability because of his or her disability. This law applies to organizations with 15 or more employees.

Reasonable accommodation is a modification or adjustment to a job, the work environment, or the way things are usually done during the hiring process. Employers should work with individuals to come up with reasonable ways of adjusting jobs and/or processes without causing the employer undue hardship.

Expand Access

The Concept of Equal Opportunity Employment.

Equal opportunity ensures people are treated the same regardless of differences. This means not basing decisions off race, age, citizenship, FMLA entitlement, veteran status, and other factors. The Equal Employment Opportunity Commission (EEOC) enforces these regulations. Basically, employment decisions must be job related. Period.

Quick history lesson: Title VII of the Civil Rights Act of 1964 was the nation's first detailed law making it illegal to discriminate in employment based on race, color, religion, sex, or national origin. There are now a number of additional areas included in federally protected classes.

Make Room for Baby

The **Pregnancy Discrimination Act (PDA)** of 1978 amended Title VII to prohibit discrimination on the basis of pregnancy, childbirth, or related medical conditions; it requires employers to treat pregnancy the same as any temporary disability.

It is illegal to....

- Refuse to hire a woman simply because she is pregnant

- Fire a woman simply because she is pregnant

- Force a pregnant employee to leave work because she is pregnant despite being willing and able to perform job duties.

- Stop the accrued tenure of an employee who has taken leave to give birth or have an abortion (unless tenure does not accrue to other temporarily disabled workers under similar circumstances)

Identity

It is important to understand the difference in these terms to avoid discrimination, harassment, and disrespect in the workplace. For example, the wording you use during onboarding can seem discriminatory if it is not specific. Simply asking someone to identify their gender vs sex can have two different meanings.

- **Sex** – This is a person's sexual anatomy, organs, and hormonal make-up. How they were born.

- **Gender** – This is how a person feels about themselves. This is how a person self- identifies.

- **Gender identity** – one's internal, personal sense of being a man or woman, which may or may not be the same as one's sexual assignment at birth. It may also be the perception by others and includes a person's appearance, behavior, or physical characteristics etc.

- **Sexual orientation** – the sexual, romantic, or emotional feelings. When we talk about being gay, straight, bisexual, etc we are referring to a person's sexual orientation.

Bully, Bye!

No one likes a bully at work. The EEOC describes harassment as unlawful for the following situations described.

- When offensive conduct becomes a condition of continued employment.

- When the conduct is severe or pervasive enough to create a work environment that a reasonable person would consider intimidating, hostile, or abusive.

- When an individual is harassed in retaliation for filing a discrimination charge, testifying, or participating in any way in an investigation, proceeding, or lawsuit.

While these are not all the rules and regulations, this is a good foundation to help you understand the ins and out when creating a safe, creative, and great place to work. Remember to always seek legal advice to ensure compliance in these areas.

Ei-Ei-OH!

Don't Forget About the E&I in Diversity, Equity, and Inclusion

Three is Not a Crowd

When it comes to diversity, equity, and inclusion you need all three. You cannot just focus on one piece and forget about the other. Let's talk about having a diverse workforce that provides inclusion to people of all abilities and backgrounds while promoting workplace equity.

Diversity

Diversity is the mix of cultures, races, genders, economic statuses, ideas, and other characteristics. By observing someone you may be able to point out visible diversity. However, when discussing diversity, it is important to consider the difference between visible and invisible diversity:

Visible diversity are characteristics that we can hear or see. Such as someone's accent when they speak or language. You can also see differences in skin tone, gender, age, and other physical traits are generally external.

Invisible diversity traits include things that typically cannot be seen or heard. This can include socioeconomic status, values, working-styles, beliefs and perspectives on certain things.

Equity vs. Equality

The term "equity" often is discussed with D&I. The word has several meanings in the world of business, however, so some clarity of its meaning in this particular context can be helpful.

- In finance, equity (almost always) means ownership or possessing something.

- In compensation, equity (almost always) means relative fairness in total rewards.

- In hiring, equity means equal opportunity (to work).

Equity does not mean providing everyone the same level of support (that's equality), instead equity is providing people the specific support they need so everyone ends up at the same playing field. Just think of something that you are really good in and don't need a lot of training versus someone who is new in the field. If the both of you were provided the same type of training you would not end up on the same playing field because different levels of support are needed.

Warm Welcome or Cold Candor?

Do your employees feel welcomed, are they glad to work for your company?

You can have a diverse company but if people do not feel included or have the support they need; it is pointless.

Inclusion is when everyone is included, welcomed, supported, respected, and valued. Here are some things to consider for driving diversity, equity, and inclusion.

- What size is your organization and what is your projected head count for the next year?

- What are your current issues with DEI? Thinking about this will help you break down barriers and have a baseline for current issues.

- How often do you discuss DEI and what does the conversation look like? Is it through email, roundtable discussions or not discussed at all?

- Is DEI something you are passionate about or do you have expertise creating a DEI strategy? You need both to implement and sustain an effective plan.

Stay Curious

Don't try to build a culture of diversity, equity, and inclusion; it will feel fake at best. Instead build a culture of curiosity, open-mindedness and respect; and inclusion will follow. We are human and all want that sense of belonging. Think about what that means in your workplace and create a culture that mirrors your mission and values.

- Get insight from other people on your team to make sure you have different perspectives.

- Discuss your pay and promotion practices.

- Build upon your company's initiatives and goals.

- Review often to ensure that policies are aligned with company efforts.

- Lead by example so policies are a true reflection of company culture, mission and strategies.

What's Your Why?

Look to other companies and see what they have done well in supporting underrepresented groups. Companies like DiversityINC, CEO Action for Diversity & Inclusion, and Seramount are great resources to support initial DEI efforts. There are many great resources and companies to benchmark, but remember your company's DEI journey is unique. It is not a one size fit all approach. Start by asking yourself: Why are we making DEI a priority for our business? Once you know your "why," everything else will likely follow.

Let's Get Awkward:

Employee Relations

Are You Serious?!

Employee relations can get interesting to say the least. Let's take a brief pause to laugh at some funny but true employee relations stories.

- An employee warms up fish in the microwave every Tuesday and other employees complain. How do you address this?

- Employee is a great worker but has bad body odor. What would you say?

- What about an employee who literally cries anytime constructive criticism is given?

Unfortunately, I have experienced all of these. It's funny now but wasn't at the moment. When managing a team, it's important to have the skills to have awkward conversations. Let's get into it!

Crucial Convos

Keep your cool amid chaos

I led a training workshop based on the Crucial Conversations program. It's a great resource for having conversations when the stakes are high.

Whether that's performance improvement conversations or discussing body odor. It's about having respect and always tying your conversation back to company culture, mission, standards, expectations and policies. Having empathy, being direct and consistent are key.

- Have conversations in a private setting to not embarrass someone.

- Allow the employee to express how they feel.

- It's not what you say, it's how you say it. Both sides need to be respectful with words, body language and tone.

Think Before You Tweet

Not too long-ago employers were able to decide how to manage employee's behavior based on what happened in the workplace. With the advanced use of social media, the line between personal and public information has blurred. The workplace is now stretched past the walls of the office. Yet, employers still have an obligation to protect employees while upholding company mission and values.

Employers have the right to prohibit discrimination, harassment, threats of violence, and may terminate those employees who behaviors violate the company's mission and values.

- Several states such as California and New York have privacy laws that prohibit employers from interfering into their employees' lives outside of work. These laws prohibit employers from firing employees for legal off-duty conduct. Unfortunately, it's not illegal to be racist but that does not mean employers cannot act.

- Send a message to your employees that you are an employer of inclusion, not exclusion.

- Create company policies that upstand your company's values, prohibit discrimination, and uphold other ethical standards.

Free Speech?

Employees have the right to free speech and protected by the National Labor Relations Act (NLRA), but to an extent. When an employee's actions have negative impacts on the workplace and go against company policy then action can be taken. The threat of a lawsuit may make employers fearful or unaware of what to do when an employee's negative behaviors impact the workplace. In the case an employee threatens with a lawsuit:

- Understand the risk, examine the situation, and remember your company culture.

- Let the employee know that due to their behaviors this is not the workplace for them (if the employee has acted in a way that negatively impacts business).

- If it does turn into a legal situation, you have your company policies, ethics, and documentation to defend your decision in court.

Keeping someone around that is discriminatory or behaves in a way that negatively impacts employees is very damaging. In the long run, your employees will appreciate the standup approach you took which will have positive impacts on your organization and employer brand.

Work Life Harmony

I get inspired by so many people but it really hit me when Jasmin Forts, owner of a Sisters Siesta mentioned work life harmony instead of work life balance. Work life balance implies that everything in your life is equal, in reality that may not be the case. Work life harmony is something leaders must promote in the workplace. Making sure mental health, family, work, and so on are properly maintained. While workshops and resources are helpful; reviewing workloads and encouraging time-off can be just what your team needs.

Remember, work-life harmony will mean different things to different people because we all have different life commitments.

Listen to your team by:

- Being supportive by knowing what your employees are striving for.

- Set a good example. Don't be that boss that sends emails all through the night.

- Remind employees what their options are.

- Stay updated on trends. What works today may look different next year or next month!

Overloaded

A good way to review workloads is through consistent one on one meetings because you can review tasks and prioritize projects. As a manager, you may not have control over timelines, but you do have control over employee workloads. Having conversations about priorities and tasks, can help manage projects, improve productivity and quality of work.

If you have an employee who is having issues completing projects on time; analyze potential roadblocks and find ways to remove those obstacles. Work together to create a plan that enables employees to meet goals and expectations. Consider employees' strong points and assign tasks accordingly.

DID YOU KNOW:

According to the 2021 Harvard Business Review, collaborative work — time spent on email, IM, phone, and video calls — has risen 50% or more over the past decade to consume 85% or more of most people's work weeks. If a meeting is necessary, make the most of it by having an agenda, takeaways, and action items. Make sure you are providing your team enough time to actually get the work done.

Digital Downtime

"I can make you put your phone down"-Erykah Badu

It can be hard to tap out of technology, especially when working from home. Work is integrated into employees' home life. Continually working through lunch breaks does not make employees more productive, it causes burn out. There will be an occasional tight deadline, but it is so important to have time to refresh and reflect.

Getting some fresh air, taking a walk or listening to some music can help employees relax and come back to work refreshed. A company I worked with had 15-minute virtual dance parties. It was corny but fun. Virtual dance party with the HR director at 3pm. Visuals I will never forget LOL.

Find something fun that works for your team and company culture. The importance is to have options available and encourage good welfare. Every organization needs to promote work-life harmony to improve health and well-being for the team. Because, when you go above and beyond for your team you encourage others to show up as their best selves

But Can I Trust You?

Ok, can we talk about trust again because that's how important it is.

Trust is vital for building productivity in the workplace. Having structure is important. Having freedom to complete work with trust and respect makes people feel good about the work they do. Having a strong hiring process can help with hiring a solid trusted person to do the job. Maintaining trust throughout the employment relationship is a key element for a better working relationship. Here are some pointers:

1. Acknowledging other people's emotions: Simply acknowledge how someone is feeling, even if you don't agree can help form deeper connections. "Hey, you seem upset" shows that you are coming from a place of care and concern. It's about how you ask and the setting. Don't impose.

2. Be clear and honest. Don't sugarcoat situations. Be real about the good and bad.

3. Treat employees like people. Situations arise. Show compassion to gain employee loyalty. Accept strengths and weaknesses, we all have them. Be a coach and help employees strengthen their weaknesses.

4. Set and example and provide guidance. Trust is built when an employee is falling but you are there to step up and support. Look through crisis and challenges and support your team.

What You Say?!

Did you take my eraser? DID YOU TAKE MY ERASER?

Did you read those messages in different tones? I said the same thing but how it was written changes the tone.

Miscommunication happens in a virtual environment because of how things are translated. Communication etiquette allows for better conversation among your team.

Virtual Communication Etiquette

- If you're sending a sensitive message. Reread it to yourself before sending. Remove email recipients to avoid accidentally sending before you are ready.

- Modes of communication. If something is urgent, do you send a email or ping? When going through collaborative meetings is it through a zoom call or a conference call?

- Set boundaries so even if you send emails late night or early mornings; employees are only expected to respond during office hours. Clear communication are important so creating communication guidelines for responding to requests and emails helps employees understand expectations.

Shock Factor

Employee relations and the changing workplace

Communication mishaps are inevitable. We may be sharing our cameras instead of meeting in person.

Providing your team with tips and best practices for communication etiquette can allow your team to work together even better.

No matter how much experience you have managing a team, you will still be shocked by some of the things that come up in the workplace. As time progresses you will become better at how you handle these situations. Pay attention to trends that effect the workplace, listen to your employees and get comfortable having difficult conversations. As a leader it is important to be consistent and compliant with what you enforce while having empathy, self-awareness and being human.

Performance Management

Let's Talk

There's many back and forth, ongoing debates around performance reviews. If performance reviews only happen once or twice per year, they will undoubtedly be ineffective. Performance management is an ongoing process. Marcus Buckingham, created a tool called **Standout** which measures employees' strengths and promotes consistent employee manager communication. We used Standout at ADP and it was a simple but effective tool that created dashboards and quick insight for my manager to see my highs and lows of the week along with other important work details. So when we had our one on one meetings we already had a foundation for our conversation. When employees and managers are having regular conversations about projects, goals and expectations performance can be measured more accurately.

Structured conversations around performance measurements need to be had, but it's also those routine one on one conversations that provide foundation for quality performance.

Make it Matter

Convos that count

Before you can implement a performance review process, you have to create a meaningful review that captures relevant information. Performance reviews help spot trends in performance and opportunities for improvement. A study conducted by Mark Murphy from LeadershipIQ found that only 13% of employees and managers think their company's appraisal system is useful. 88% of respondents said their current performance process negatively affects their view of HR. What did HR do?! That's a different convo but let's stay on track.

Create a review that correctly assesses performance and goals. Before creating a review, ask yourself;

- What is the objective?

- What should we measure to get an accurate view of an employee's performance and progression?

- What are the key performance indicators (KPI's). KPI's need to have a number attached to be measurable.

Ask Right

Before creating questions, think about a broader category of employee qualities you want to measure.

- **Problem Solving**: Does this employee look for creative problem-solving approaches?

- **Leadership**: Does this person often lead team initiatives and projects?

- **Communication**: Does this person have a positive attitude and interact well with co-workers?

- **Effort**: Does this employee put forth quality effort in their work?

- **Relevance**: Questions need to be relevant to an employee's role, goals, and reflect the reality of their work.

Ask questions that allow employees to think about their performance and highlight their best assets.

Performance Reviews are about giving feedback so employees can grow and improve. Employees may find the review useless if they are not receiving any helpful feedback. Make sure you provide a clear purpose for assessing performance and how you will follow up.

What's the Vibe?

Your attitude, tone, and body language set the vibe for performance conversations. Create a welcoming environment where information can be openly discussed.

Communication is part of everything. Ask your managers and employees how they feel about performance reviews so you can talk through difficulties and assist where needed. Maybe a manager has trouble giving difficult feedback or maybe they are having trouble setting aside time to conduct multiple reviews. Talk to your team about issues so you can provide the right resources.

Yes, performance reviews should have structure but do not make it a bland process. When you add the words" process or procedures" to some things it can sound "stuffy". Be creative, call the review what you would like long as it's getting done!

Skills: To Do Something Great

Offer employees unique learning and development opportunities to gain skills for their careers. It's a win a win. Employees are reaching career milestones while increasing job knowledge. Employees do not want to feel closed in and bored with their position. Even if skill development does not include an upward move in positions, it still offers employees the opportunity to grow. Something as simple as leading a meeting develops communication and directive skills. It also provides an employee a sense of ownership.

When it comes to skill development having structure is important but it also needs to be enjoyable. Going through a basic PowerPoint slideshow is not the way! Consider various ways your team learns and discover ways to implement those options.

Knowledge Gap

Close the knowledge gap by implementing creative ways for learning.

- **Mentorship**- Having a one-on-one mentoring program helps employees learn specific details about a position. It is also important to create a culture of mentorship where everyone is encouraged to help each other grow.

- **Microlearning**- Breaking information down in small sections can help employees grasp information easier. Employees need to be able to apply skills learned to the work they do. on the job. Micro learning combined with on-the-job training turns skills into real capabilities.

- **Managers** play a huge role in skill development. Managers can become better coaches by learning about each employee and help guide them on their path to success.

Skills To Win The Deal

"Soft skills are essential to the future of work" -Forbes

Think of soft skills as essential skills. As Alan Weiss would say, language builds discussions and discussions build relationships. The ability to collaborate and communicate is one of the most important skills a company can promote. Include essential skills in your performance reviews so employees can see metrics on what this kind of development looks like.

Be Aware of Your Own Bias

Although bias is part of being human, it can negatively impact the ability to evaluate performance. Sometimes bias happens without even recognizing it. Being aware of your own bias equips you to be a better employee, manager and/or leader. It also helps with accuracy in the review process. Cultural differences, stereotypes and leaders' past experiences can all contribute to rater bias. If you have an employee with autism, a manager may stereotype neurodivergent individuals. With the proper training, leaders can improve their management style by understanding their basis and having knowledge to manage diverse teams. The Job Accommodation Network is a great resource for training. Also speaking directly with your team members and find what works best.

Smart Risk

Smart Risk

Taking risk is part of business and part of your role as a leader. Deciding what technology to implement, what training and development resource to push out, even who to hire.

Managing risk in a skillful way helps a company benefit and develops your skills as a leader. Taking risk and being able to pivot in unforeseen circumstances requires the right knowledge, agility, resources and support. To take smart risk, be sure to understand your company ways of working, goals for the future, and always use the mission and vision as a compass.

Did You Know?

The International Organization for Standardization (ISO) released Standard 3100 as a guide for taking business risks. ISO defines risk management as "coordinated activities to direct and control an organization with regard to risk.

Identifying Risk

Duty of care means that the organization takes all reasonable steps to ensure the health, safety and well-being of workers by protecting from foreseeable injuries. It spans the entire employment relationship and sometimes beyond into retirement. In some cultures, it extends to the employees' families. How can your organization improve its understanding of risk?

- Focus groups and individual interviews

- Surveys

- Process analysis

- Direct observation

- Consulting experts and information sources

Drug Use

But its legal,
what can I do?

Symptoms and risks posed by drug use may appear regardless of whether the use occurred before, during, or after work. A lot of questions with medical marijuana (MMJ) have been raised in the workplace. Although MMJ use is legal in some states, employers still have the right to prohibit the use and influence while at work. Just as alcohol is legal, but cannot be used at work. The same goes for medical marijuana; even if used for medical reasons. Even if use was outside of work, the symptoms of drug use can pose risk at work.

- Less productivity

- Property Damage

- Risk to others (EX: operating machines while under the influence).

Writing organizational policies regarding performance, discipline, and rehabilitation can empower managers to act more rapidly and confidently to suspected drug abuse issues. Training and education is also important for mitigating risk.

Stay Ready

That's why I stay ready- Jhene Aiko

Prepare for the worst but hope for the best. Stay ready so you don't have to get ready. I am not implying for you to be negative and pessimistic, but understand the ins and outs of your business so you can prepare for various incidents.

Security Threats

- Cybersecurity threats
- Physical security risk such as workplace violence

Illness and Injury

- Physical health hazards include vibration, smoking, sanitary condition, workplace design, etc.
- Chemical health hazards include gases, toxic materials, smoke, etc.

Comp & Bennys

Where the Bag at?

What does competitive pay *really* mean.

So many employers claim to offer "competitive pay", but what is competitive pay?

Depending on the industry or job, competitive pay can vary. Using tools like Glassdoor or Indeed can provide pay benchmarking details.

Advanced benchmarking resources provide compensation details based on location, experience, company size, and more. Regardless of what resource you utilize, its important to have a solid compensation strategy to attract and keep the best players. Be sure to align pay with internal pay standards to ensure equity.

Add It Up

While there are various types of compensation, typically most people want to know about direct compensation.

- Hourly
- Salary
- Commission
- Bonuses

Highlight direct compensation first and foremost, but do not forget to mention other forms of compensation. Indirect compensation includes paid time off and benefits. Direct and indirect compensation make up the total compensation package and include equity, benefits, and taxes paid by employers on the employee's behalf.

Direct compensation includes:

- Base salary
- Wages
- Bonuses
- Commission
- Overtime

Indirect compensation includes:

- Insurance (health, dental, vision, etc.)
- Paid leave (vacations, holidays, sick days, etc.)
- Retirement contributions
- Career development programs Tuition reimbursement
- Student loan repayment assistance

Non-financial compensation can also include:

- Work-life programs
- Company volunteerism (walking for a cause, allowing employees to take time off to volunteer for a cause of their choice)

Tokens Of Appreciation: 55 Ways To Value Your Team

If you are a small business do not think you cannot compete with big businesses in regards to providing competitive pay. There are many ways you can stand out as an employer of choice and provide attractive benefits and perks to your employees. Here is a list of over 50 different benefits and perks you can provide to your employees for a small cost.

When it comes to rewarding your team, the possibilities are endless. Get to know your team, their interest, and hobbies and create perks that matter to them. Be opened- minded, curious, and creative and you will be able to provide perks that work!

1. Providing resources like the headspace app for mental health and wellness
2. Discounted childcare
3. Discounted elder care
4. Grocery delivery
5. Lunch gift card (great idea for remote employees who can't enjoy in office pizza Friday)
6. Half day Fridays (you can do this once a month if a particular goal is achieved)
7. Tuition reimbursement
8. Reimbursement for certifications and trainings
9. Wellness challenges
10. Rewards for going above and beyond
11. Highlight an employee each week during team meeting
12. Team shoutouts: Place where team members can give thanks to other team members
13. Volunteer days
14. Gym membership discount
15. Financial assistance

16. Office decor stipend
17. Work from a home resource basket (pens, company swag, mug, tshirt, etc.)
18. Team catered lunch
19. Flex time options
20. Pay it Forward (did you land hard to get reservations at a restaurant, pass it team member)
21. to get into management)
22. Escape room team building events (this can be done virtual as well!)
23. Have a trainer come into the office (We had a trainer from Dale Carnegie come in.)
24. Put together a team cookbook with recipes from team members then send it out to everyone.
25. Handwritten thank you note
26. Photo shoot (hire a local photographer to provide company headshots)
27. Partnering with local organizations to bring business to their organization in exchange for employee discounts. (For example, partner with a local coffee shop to provide 10% employee discount.)
28. Stock options
29. Equipped office kitchen (great perk for companies who have in office employees)
30. Employee of the month reward
31. Home buying assistance (partner with a local real estate branch)
32. Company-wide off day for mental health
33. Trendy office lounge
34. Hire a mobile car detailing company to come to your office and provide discounts for car washes
35. Tickets to a local sporting event
36. Host a company BBQ
37. Virtual cookie contest (send your team a cookie decorating kit with pre-made cookies and set the timer for who makes the best decorated cookie. Great idea for remote staff.).
38. Virtual trivia on important details about the company and roles
39. Extend invitation to an executive meeting

40. Employee Discounts
41. Quarterly Contest for best themed home office (Contest for the best tropical themed office)
42. Share accomplishments on internal wall of fame
43. Fuel gift card
44. Stipend for internet
45. Stipend for phone bill
46. Partner with a cleaning company to provide discounts on house cleaning in exchange for business referrals. (This can be really helpful for remote employees who spend more time at home.)
47. Hire a food truck to come to the office. (Set up a few tables and enjoy lunch outside during a warm day.)
48. Employee Assistance Program (A quality EAP can help with a variety of tasks from help with finding daycares to mental health resources.)
49. Virtual Comedy Show
50. Discounted co-working space (Think about places like WeWork. This can be beneficial for remote employees who are not near a company office.)
51. Become a learning partner with a college to provide discounted tuition.
52. Pet insurance
53. Voluntary benefits
54. Celebrating fun holidays (April 1st is international fun day at work day.)
55. Gamification (when done correctly can be very beneficial)

That's A Wrap...

I can do this for hours...

I can go on and on but I'll save it for another time. This journey was fun and I am so grateful to share my knowledge with you.

When it comes to managing a team, don't get caught up with having all the answers. You never will. The best thing you can do to manage a great team is encourage open- mindedness, provide coaching, promote creativity and over communicate. Take time to get to know employees and prove that you care. In return you will have a group of people that support your business, team and ideas with honesty and respect. Employee loyalty is developed when you consistently show up and lead from within. You already proven that you care because you're here. Now you have new ideas and perspectives for creating a great place to work. Keep this guide close for building and managing your solid team.

You got this!

Resources

Bottoroff, C. (2022). Where to post your jobs to find the best candidates. https://www.forbes.com/advisor/business/where-to-post-jobs/

Bostock, J. In the war for talent, competition has never been so fierce. (2021). https://www.forbes.com/sites/forbesbusinesscouncil/2021/07/20/in-the-war-for-talent-competition-has-never-been-so-fierce/?sh=669b2ba4118b

Brower, T. The future of work and the new workplace: how to make work better. https://www.forbes.com/sites/tracybrower/2021/02/07/the- future-of-work-and-the-new-workplace-how-to-make-work-better/?sh=3acbb4a7450a. T

Bureau of Labor Statistics. (2022). News release bureau of labor statistics employment situation. https://www.bls.gov/news.release/pdf/empsit.pdf

Daft, L.R. (2020). Organization theory & design. (13th ed.). Cengage learning.

Deloitte (sponsored content). (2019). Why your organization's future demands a new kind of HR. https://hbr.org/sponsored/2019/02/why-your-organizations-future-demands-a-new-kind-of-hr

Emmer, M. (2021). Five secrets to finding talent. https://www.forbes.com/sites/forbesbusinesscouncil/2021/08/26/five-secrets-to-finding-talent/? sh=36ee40ed9398

Fuller,B., Manjari, R., Gavin, S.E., Hines, K. (2021). Hidden workers: untapped talent. https://www.hbs.edu/managing-the-future-of-work/Documents/research/hiddenworkers09032021.pdf

Ganzert, R. Four key tips for cultivating a positive work environment. https://www.forbes.com/sites/forbesnonprofitcouncil/2022/01/04/four-key- tips-for-cultivating-a-positive-work-environment/?sh=6e4f4a0330ff.

Govindji, K. (2022). 6 ways to help your dei initiatives drive greater impact. https://www.forbes.com/sites/googlecloud/2022/02/10/6-ways-to- help-your-dei-initiatives-driver-greater-impact/?sh=196e16452eec

Heneman, H. G. (2021). Staffing Organizations (10th Edition). McGraw-Hill Higher Education (US). https://mbsdirect.vitalsource.com/books/9781264072590

London Business School. (2021). Managing in a virtual workplace-making use of all possible levers of influence. https://www.forbes.com/sites/lbsbusinessstrategyreview/2021/07/16/man aging-in-a-virtual-workplacemaking-use-of-all-possible-levers-of-influence/?sh=241e7b6c14c2

MacArthur, H.V. (2021). HR's new role: how human resources need to evolve to support the future of work. https://www.forbes.com/sites/hvmacarthur/2021/03/18/hrs-new-role-how-human-resources-needs-to-evolve-to-support-the-future-of-work/?sh=4fa4b62a3bc1

N.A. (N.D). Misclassification of employees as independent contractors. https://www.dol.gov/agencies/whd/flsa/misclassification

Perna, M. (2021) 5 Huge companies are contributing to their own talent shortage. https://www.forbes.com/sites/markcperna/2022/04/19/5-huge-ways-companies-are-contributing-to-their-own-talent-shortage/?sh=711f39b659fa.

Sparkman, R. (2018). Strategic workforce planning. Kogan Page.

Zgola, M. (2021). Will the gig economy become the new working-class norm? https://www.forbes.com/sites/forbesbusinesscouncil/2021/08/12/will-the-gig-economy-become-the-new-working-class-norm/?sh=74e96205aee6

The secret to success is not a secret. Be intentional about hiring, leading, and developing others. A solid team is what takes your business to THE next level.

Cheers to success,
Shayna Robinson
www.HowToHR.org

www.ingramcontent.com/pod-product-compliance
Lightning Source LLC
Chambersburg PA
CBHW050619210326
41521CB00008B/1318